RESTORATIVE JUSTICE FOR JUVENILES

Dr. Maxwell Shimba

Copyright © 2023 – Dr. Maxwell Shimba

All rights reserved. No portion of this book may be reproduced, stored in a retrieval system, or transmitted in any form or by any means – electronics, mechanical, photocopy, recording, scanning, or other – except for brief quotations in critical reviews or articles, without the prior written permission of the publisher.

Published in Manhattan, New York by Shimba Publishing, LLC.

Shimba Publishing LLC

Printed in the United States of America

First Printing Edition, 2023

TABLE OF CONTENTS

- Introduction vi
- Chapter 01 1
- The Concept of Restorative Justice for Juveniles 1
- Chapter 02 6
- Historical Contexed Juvenile Justice 6
- Chapter 03 11
- Principles of Restorative Justice 11
- Chapter 04 17
- Victim-Centered approach 17
- Chapter 05 21
- Offender Rehabilitation 21
- Chapter 06 27
- Community Involvement 27
- Chapter 07 35
- Restorative Practices 35
- Chapter 08 45
- Benefits of Restorative Justice 45
- Chapter 09 52
- Challenges and Criticism 52
- Chapter 10 60
- Legal Framework 60
- Chapter 11 65
- Case Studies 65
- Chapter 12 70
- Restorative Justice Worldwide 70
- Chapter 13 76
- Future Directions 76

Chapter 14	82
Practical Guidance	82
Chapter 15	89
Conclusion	89

INTRODUCTION

In the intricate tapestry of the criminal justice system, a profound transformation is underway—one that places healing, accountability, and community at its core. At the heart of this transformation lies the concept of restorative justice for juveniles, a path less traveled but of profound significance.

This book embarks on a journey to uncover the essence and significance of restorative justice in the context of young offenders. It shines a light on its pivotal role in redefining the way we address juvenile delinquency, emphasizing rehabilitation over retribution. Throughout these pages, we will delve into the fundamental principles that underpin this approach, explore the innovative practices that give it life, and bear witness to the numerous benefits it brings to our communities.

As we navigate this exploration, it becomes evident that restorative justice for juveniles is not just a concept—it is a compass pointing toward a more compassionate and effective future within the criminal justice landscape. It is an approach that values second chances, empowers victims, and reshapes the destinies of young individuals who have strayed off course. Join us on this transformative journey as we unravel the intricate tapestry of restorative justice for juveniles.

RJ For Juveniles

DR. MAXWELL SHIMBA

CHAPTER 01

THE CONCEPT OF RESTORATIVE JUSTICE FOR JUVENILES

In the world of juvenile justice, a transformative approach has emerged, one that shifts the focus from punitive measures to healing and accountability. This book sets out on a journey to unravel the essence of restorative justice for juveniles, a concept that has gained recognition for its profound impact on the criminal justice system. As we navigate these pages, we will delve into the core principles, innovative practices, and multifaceted benefits that restorative justice offers to young offenders. It is a system that believes in second chances, in rebuilding lives, and in forging stronger, more empathetic communities. This book aims to shed light on how restorative justice can reshape the future of our youth within the criminal justice landscape.

The concept of restorative justice for juveniles is rooted in the belief that when a young individual commits an offense, the primary focus should not be solely on punishment but on repairing the harm caused to victims and communities. This approach is based on several key principles, practices, and benefits that distinguish it from traditional punitive methods within the criminal justice system.

Principles of Restorative Justice for Juveniles:

1. Accountability: Restorative justice holds young offenders accountable for their actions by encouraging them to acknowledge the harm they've caused and take responsibility for their behavior.

2. Empathy: It fosters empathy in young offenders by allowing them to understand the impact of their actions on victims, as well as the broader community, thereby promoting personal growth and understanding.

3. Community Involvement: Community members play a crucial role in restorative justice processes. They participate in dialogues, circles, or conferences, helping to

address the harm caused by the offense and providing support for both victims and offenders.

Practices in Restorative Justice for Juveniles:

1. Victim-Offender Dialogues: These structured conversations bring together victims and young offenders, facilitated by a trained mediator. It allows victims to express their feelings, ask questions, and, ideally, reach an agreement for restitution or other forms of redress.

2. Restorative Circles: Circles involve victims, offenders, and community members in a collaborative and structured dialogue. They provide a space for open communication, understanding, and conflict resolution.

3. Restorative Conferences: Conferences are more formal gatherings that bring together all affected parties, including victims, offenders, their supporters, and relevant community members. They discuss the offense, and its consequences, and develop a plan for restitution or reconciliation.

Benefits of Restorative Justice for Juveniles:

1. Reduced Recidivism: Restorative justice programs have been shown to reduce reoffending rates among young offenders. By addressing the root causes of delinquency and fostering personal growth, they can break the cycle of criminal behavior.

2. Improved Victim Satisfaction: Victims often find more satisfaction and closure in restorative justice processes, as they have a direct say in how the offender makes amends. This contrasts with traditional court proceedings, where victims may feel marginalized.

3. Stronger Communities: Restorative justice promotes community involvement and engagement, leading to safer and more cohesive neighborhoods. It builds trust, encourages cooperation, and addresses the underlying issues that contribute to juvenile crime.

Procedural justice theory posits that juveniles are more inclined to comply with the law when they perceive the criminal justice system as a reasonable and legitimate institution (Tyler, 1994). This concept is grounded in the belief that an individual's sense of fairness regarding the outcomes they experience within the justice system significantly influences their perception of law enforcement, their adherence to legal norms, and, ultimately, their propensity to engage in re-offending (Hipple, Gruenewald, and McGarrell, 2014).

Empirical research has consistently shown that restorative justice programs are generally perceived as more legitimate compared to conventional criminal justice procedures (Hayes and Daly, 2003; Kuo, Longmire, and

Cuvelier, 2010). Restorative justice, therefore, represents a fusion of two key elements: reintegrative shaming and procedural justice. It accomplishes this by involving the public in a transparent justice process intentionally designed to foster healing, or the "restoration," of the justice-involved youth, the victim, and the wider community.

CHAPTER 02

HISTORICAL CONTEXED JUVENILE JUSTICE

The historical context of restorative justice for juveniles is rooted in the evolution of the juvenile justice system. Historically, young offenders were often treated in the same punitive manner as adult criminals, facing harsh penalties and confinement. This approach, however, had significant shortcomings. It failed to account for the unique vulnerabilities and potential for rehabilitation among young individuals, often perpetuating cycles of criminality.

Restorative justice emerged as an alternative in response to these shortcomings. It gained prominence as a philosophy and practice in the latter half of the 20th century. This paradigm shift was influenced by a growing recognition that punitive measures alone did not address the underlying causes of juvenile delinquency or promote community safety. Restorative justice offered a more holistic approach, emphasizing accountability, victim-offender dialogue, and community involvement as key elements in the rehabilitation of young offenders. It recognized that addressing harm and fostering empathy could lead to more meaningful and lasting resolutions for both victims and juveniles in conflict with the law. This shift in perspective marked a pivotal moment in the history of juvenile justice, paving the way for a more compassionate and effective approach.

Furthermore, historical background of juvenile justice is a complex tapestry that has evolved over centuries. In ancient societies, juveniles who committed offenses were often treated similarly to adults and subjected to harsh punishments. It wasn't until the late 19th century that the concept of a separate juvenile justice system began to take shape.

The early juvenile justice system, which emerged in the late 19th and early 20th centuries in the United States, was rooted in the belief that young offenders were more amenable to rehabilitation than adult criminals. The system focused on providing guidance, counseling, and education to help young individuals reintegrate into society as responsible citizens. The emphasis was on treating juveniles as "wards of the court" rather than as criminals.

Despite its initial promise, the traditional punitive approach to juvenile justice had several significant shortcomings:

1. Stigmatization: Young offenders were often stigmatized and labeled as delinquents, which could have a lasting negative impact on their lives and hinder their rehabilitation.

2. Incarceration: In some cases, juveniles were placed in the same facilities as adult criminals, exposing them to the influence of hardened criminals and potentially increasing the likelihood of reoffending.

3. Lack of Due Process: The early system lacked procedural safeguards and due process rights for juveniles, leading to potential abuses and unfair treatment.

4. Limited Accountability: The system did not always hold juveniles accountable for their actions, which could lead to a lack of understanding and responsibility for the harm they caused.

The shortcomings of the traditional punitive approach to juvenile justice eventually led to the emergence of restorative justice as a compelling alternative. Restorative justice gained traction in the latter half of the 20th century as a response to the limitations of punitive methods. It offered a more holistic and compassionate approach to addressing juvenile delinquency by focusing on the following key principles:

1. Accountability: Restorative justice emphasizes that young offenders should take responsibility for their actions, acknowledge the harm they've caused, and actively work towards making amends.

2. Empathy: It fosters empathy in both victims and offenders, encouraging them to understand each other's perspectives and needs.

3. Community Involvement: Restorative justice actively involves the community in the resolution process, recognizing that addressing harm requires collective effort.

In the context of a conventional justice system, professionals often approach cases by asking questions centered on the nature of the law's violation, like "What laws have been broken?" and "What punishment should be assigned to the convicted juvenile?" However, within the restorative justice model, the framing of these inquiries takes a different form, with a focus on understanding the harm caused by the crime. Questions such as "What is the nature of the harm resulting from the crime?" and "What actions are necessary to repair this harm?" become central (National Center for Mental Health Promotion and Youth Violence, 2009).

From a restorative justice standpoint, the process of rehabilitation is contingent upon the justice-involved youth acknowledging the harm they have caused and taking steps to make amends (Bazemore and Umbreit, 1997). Restorative justice programs operate by bringing together not only the victims and the justice-involved youths but also community members and other key stakeholders in various settings. This approach aims to help the youths gain a deeper understanding of the consequences of their actions and provides them with an opportunity to reestablish connections within the community. Achieving both of these goals holds the potential to reduce the likelihood of reoffending (Zehr, 2002; Braithwaite, 2002; Strang et al., 2013).

CHAPTER 03

PRINCIPLES OF RESTORATIVE JUSTICE

The principles of restorative justice for juveniles form the cornerstone of this transformative approach. Three key principles stand out: accountability, empathy, and community involvement.

Accountability in restorative justice emphasizes that young offenders should take responsibility for their actions. Unlike traditional punitive methods that often rely solely on punishment, restorative justice encourages juveniles to understand the consequences of their behavior and make amends to those they have harmed. It shifts the focus from punitive retribution to making things right.

Empathy is another critical principle. In restorative justice, there is a deep emphasis on fostering empathy in both the offenders and the victims. Juveniles are encouraged to see the human face of their actions and understand the impact they've had on others. This contrasts starkly with punitive methods that often dehumanize offenders, making rehabilitation and reintegration into society more challenging.

Community involvement is the third principle, recognizing that the broader community plays a vital role in the juvenile's rehabilitation. Restorative justice actively engages the community in the process, seeking to mend the social fabric torn by the offense. This involvement helps create a supportive environment for the young offender to reintegrate successfully.

In contrast to traditional punitive methods that isolate offenders from the community and focus primarily on punishment, restorative justice aligns these principles to provide a more holistic and effective approach to addressing juvenile delinquency. It promotes healing, growth, and a sense of responsibility that can lead to better outcomes for young offenders and the communities they are part of.

1. Accountability: Restorative justice places a strong emphasis on accountability. Offenders are encouraged to take responsibility for their actions, acknowledge the harm they've caused, and actively work towards making amends to those they've harmed. This accountability goes beyond mere punishment; it seeks to address the root causes of the behavior and promote personal growth and change.

2. Empathy: Fostering empathy is a fundamental principle of restorative justice. It encourages both victims and offenders to see the human face of their actions. Victims have the opportunity to express the emotional and practical impact of the offense, while offenders are encouraged to understand the consequences of their behavior on a personal level. This focus on empathy aims to create a deeper understanding between the parties involved.

3. Community Involvement: Restorative justice recognizes that the harm caused by an offense extends beyond just the victim and offender; it affects the broader community. As such, community involvement is a core principle. Community members often play a role in restorative processes, providing support, guidance, and a sense of collective responsibility for addressing the harm and promoting healing.

Differences from Traditional Punitive Methods:

1. Focus on Healing Over Punishment: Restorative justice places a greater emphasis on healing, understanding, and rehabilitation rather than punitive measures. While traditional punitive methods prioritize punishment and retribution, restorative justice seeks to address the underlying causes of delinquent behavior.

2. Empathy Over Dehumanization: Restorative justice encourages empathy and understanding between victims and offenders. In contrast, traditional punitive methods often dehumanize offenders, making rehabilitation and reintegration into society more challenging.

3. Community Engagement Over Isolation: Restorative justice actively involves the community in the resolution process. Traditional punitive methods tend to isolate offenders from the community and rely solely on punishment without addressing the broader social context of their actions.

4. Long-Term Solutions Over Short-Term Fixes: Restorative justice aims to create lasting solutions by addressing the root causes of delinquency and promoting personal growth and change. Traditional punitive methods often offer short-term fixes that may not address the underlying issues contributing to criminal behavior.

Restorative justice is underpinned by two pivotal theories: reintegrative shaming (Braithwaite, 1989) and procedural justice (Tyler, 1990). Reintegrative shaming theory posits that individuals are deterred from criminal behavior through two informal types of social control: 1) their conscience and 2) the fear of facing social disapproval (Braithwaite, 1989). In restorative justice programs, justice-involved youths' actions undergo a process of "shaming" by the community before they are welcomed back into the fold. This approach counteracts the stigmatization and labeling that individuals convicted of crimes often encounter when reintegrating into society. Extensive research suggests that individuals who are embraced by the community upon reintegration are more inclined to engage in prosocial behaviors, ultimately reducing their likelihood of reoffending (Braithwaite, 1989; Liberman and Katz, 2020).

On the other hand, procedural justice theory posits that individuals are more likely to adhere to the law when they perceive the criminal justice system as a fair and legitimate institution (Tyler, 1994). This is grounded in the belief that a person's perception of fairness regarding their personal experiences within the justice system significantly influences their view of law enforcement, compliance with legal norms, and their ultimate decision to reoffend (Hipple, Gruenewald, and McGarrell, 2014). Research consistently demonstrates that restorative justice programs are generally perceived as more legitimate when compared to traditional criminal justice processes (Hayes and Daly, 2003; Kuo, Longmire, and Cuvelier, 2010).

Therefore, restorative justice effectively blends reintegrative shaming and procedural justice by engaging the public in a transparent justice process intentionally designed to facilitate healing and "restore" the justice-involved youth, the victim, and the broader community.

CHAPTER 04

VICTIM-CENTERED APPROACH

Restorative justice's victim-centered approach is a fundamental aspect that sets it apart from traditional punitive measures. This approach places the needs and rights of victims at the forefront of the justice process, recognizing their central role in addressing harm and seeking resolution.

In a victim-centered restorative justice process, victims are given the opportunity to express their feelings, concerns, and needs directly to the offender. They have a voice in determining how the offender can make amends for the harm caused, which can include restitution, apologies, or other forms of redress. This empowerment of victims can be incredibly cathartic, allowing them to regain a sense of control and closure that may be lacking in traditional criminal justice systems.

Furthermore, the victim-centered approach acknowledges that the harm caused by an offense extends beyond the immediate victim; it also affects the broader community. By involving victims and giving them a voice, restorative justice aims to repair not only the individual harm but also the social fabric that has been damaged.

In essence, the victim-centered approach of restorative justice is vital because it shifts the justice process from being solely punitive to being reparative and healing. It acknowledges the profound impact of crime on victims and seeks to provide them with a sense of justice, closure, and the opportunity for healing and recovery.

A victim-centered approach is a fundamental aspect of restorative justice, distinguishing it from traditional punitive methods in the criminal justice system. This approach places victims at the forefront, recognizing their central role in the process of addressing harm and seeking resolution. Here's how the victim-centered nature of restorative justice empowers victims to have a voice in the process:

1. Voice and Participation: Restorative justice actively involves victims in the resolution process. Victims are given the opportunity to express their feelings, concerns, and needs directly to the offender in a safe and structured setting. This engagement allows victims to have a voice in determining how the offender can make amends for the harm caused.

2. Understanding and Empowerment: Victim-centered restorative justice processes aim to help victims understand the motivations behind the offender's actions and foster empathy. This understanding can be empowering for victims, as it allows them to see the human face of the offender and may provide a sense of closure and relief.

3. Satisfaction and Healing: Traditional punitive methods often leave victims feeling marginalized and dissatisfied with the justice system's handling of their cases. In contrast, restorative justice offers victims the opportunity for satisfaction and healing by addressing their emotional and practical needs.

4. Redress and Restitution: Victim-offender dialogues in restorative justice can lead to agreements for restitution or other forms of redress. This means that victims have a direct

say in how the offender can make amends, which can be a powerful tool for restoring what was lost.

5. Closure and Moving Forward: Engaging in a restorative process can provide victims with a sense of closure and a path for moving forward after the offense. It allows them to actively participate in shaping the resolution, rather than being passive observers.

6. Preventing Re-Victimization: Victim-centered restorative justice processes aim to prevent re-victimization by ensuring that victims are treated with dignity and respect throughout the process. This approach reduces the risk of secondary trauma that can result from traditional court proceedings.

Overall, the victim-centered nature of restorative justice recognizes that the justice process should not solely be about punishment but also about addressing the needs and rights of victims. It empowers victims by giving them a voice, offering a path to healing, and providing a sense of justice that traditional punitive methods often struggle to achieve.

CHAPTER 05

OFFENDER REHABILITATION

Offender rehabilitation is a central aspect of restorative justice for young offenders. Unlike traditional punitive approaches that often focus solely on punishment and confinement, restorative justice places a strong emphasis on the idea that individuals, even young offenders, can change and grow. It seeks to rehabilitate them and facilitate their reintegration into society as responsible, law-abiding citizens.

In restorative justice processes, young offenders are encouraged to take responsibility for their actions, acknowledge the harm they've caused, and actively work towards making amends. This may involve participating in restitution, community service, or educational programs tailored to address the specific needs and circumstances of the offender.

Moreover, restorative justice often provides support and guidance to help juveniles address the underlying causes of their delinquent behavior, which can include factors such as family issues, substance abuse, or mental health challenges. By addressing these root causes, restorative justice aims to break the cycle of criminality and promote personal growth and development.

Ultimately, restorative justice recognizes that rehabilitation is not only possible but essential for the long-term well-being of young offenders and the safety of the community. It offers a path for them to learn from their mistakes, make meaningful changes in their lives, and become productive members of society once again.

Offender rehabilitation is a central aspect of restorative justice, especially when applied to young offenders. It entails a process of helping individuals who have engaged in delinquent or criminal behavior to address the underlying causes of their actions, develop pro-social skills, and reintegrate into society as responsible citizens. Restorative justice places a strong emphasis on rehabilitation, and here's how it focuses on rehabilitating young offenders and why reintegration is essential:

1. Acknowledging Responsibility: Restorative justice encourages young offenders to acknowledge their responsibility for their actions. By taking ownership of their behavior and understanding its impact on victims and the community, they begin the process of self-awareness and accountability.

2. Personal Growth and Change: Through restorative justice processes such as victim-offender dialogues and conferences, young offenders have the opportunity to reflect on their actions, their motivations, and the harm they've caused. This self-reflection can be a catalyst for personal growth and change.

3. Making Amends: Restorative justice often involves developing plans for restitution or other forms of redress to repair the harm caused. This process allows young offenders to actively take steps to make amends for their actions, contributing to their rehabilitation.

4. Addressing Underlying Factors: Restorative justice recognizes that many young offenders have underlying issues

contributing to their delinquent behavior, such as family problems, substance abuse, or mental health challenges. The process aims to address these root causes through counseling, support, and access to necessary resources.

5. Community Involvement: Community members play a significant role in restorative justice processes, offering support, mentorship, and guidance to young offenders. This community involvement provides a positive influence and a sense of belonging, which can be instrumental in rehabilitation.

6. Reintegration into Society: Restorative justice places a strong emphasis on helping young offenders reintegrate into society as responsible citizens. This reintegration is essential for reducing recidivism and ensuring that individuals do not become trapped in a cycle of criminal behavior.

Restorative justice programs typically focus on youths who have committed minor or nonviolent offenses, although some programs also extend their scope to youths involved in more serious crimes (Bradshaw, Roseborough, and Umbreit, 2006; Bouffard et al., 2017). The age range of participants can vary among programs, but generally, they encompass youths aged 11 to 17.

Research indicates that individuals convicted of different types of offenses may be directed to various restorative justice programs depending on their risk level to the community (Bergseth and Bouffard, 2012). For instance, nonviolent or younger justice-involved youths with no prior criminal history might find themselves in short-term, low-intensity programs like indirect mediation. In contrast, high-intensity programs emphasizing direct dialogues between victims and justice-involved youths, such as victim impact panels or conferences, may be reserved for youths with a history of repeated offenses or those posing a greater harm to the community (Bergseth and Bouffard, 2012; Bouffard et al., 2017).

Furthermore, restorative justice programming can intersect with justice-involved youth at different stages within the juvenile justice system, including arrest, referral, intake, and post-adjudication. Some restorative justice programs are designed as diversion options, diverting youths away from the formal justice system (Wilson, Olaghere, and Kimbrell, 2017; Silva and Plassmeyer, 2021). Others are structured as disposition outcomes, where youths are mandated to participate as part of their sentence (Wilson, Olaghere, and Kimbrell, 2017; Silva and Plassmeyer, 2021). Additionally, some restorative justice programs are voluntary, requiring participants to admit responsibility for their actions, while others are court-mandated post-adjudication (Wong et al., 2016; Pavelka and Seymour, 2019).

Lastly, restorative justice practices can be adopted within school systems as an alternative to traditional disciplinary measures such as suspension or expulsion. Statistics from the U.S. Department of Education for the 2017–18 school year reveal that out of 50.9 million students enrolled in public schools, 2.5 million students received at least one out-of-school suspension, and 101,600 students faced expulsion (Payne and Welch, 2018; U.S. Department of Education Office for Civil Rights, 2021). Restorative justice approaches serve as a means to keep students in school and substitute exclusionary discipline with more constructive alternatives.

Reintegrating young offenders as responsible citizens benefits not only the individuals themselves but also society as a whole. It reduces the likelihood of future offenses, enhances public safety, and helps create a more inclusive and compassionate community. By focusing on rehabilitation and reintegration, restorative justice offers a path for young offenders to learn from their mistakes, make meaningful changes in their lives, and become productive members of society once again.

CHAPTER 06

COMMUNITY INVOLVEMENT

Community involvement is of paramount importance in juvenile restorative practices for several compelling reasons. Firstly, it recognizes that the impact of juvenile delinquency extends beyond just the victim and offender; it affects the entire community. By actively involving the community in restorative justice processes, a sense of shared responsibility is fostered, and the community plays a vital role in addressing harm and facilitating healing.

Secondly, community involvement provides a support network for both victims and offenders. Victims often benefit from the emotional and practical support of their community as they navigate the aftermath of a crime. For young offenders, community support can be instrumental in their rehabilitation and reintegration into society. It offers guidance, mentorship, and a sense of belonging that can help steer them away from further delinquency.

Additionally, the community can provide valuable resources to aid in restitution and rehabilitation efforts. This might include educational programs, job training, or counseling services that can be accessed by young offenders as part of their restorative journey.

Overall, community involvement in juvenile restorative practices not only strengthens the bonds within the community but also enhances the effectiveness of the restorative justice process. It creates a more holistic and supportive environment where healing, growth, and accountability can flourish.

Community involvement is a vital component of restorative justice processes, and its importance cannot be overstated. The active participation of the community serves several critical roles in restorative justice and offers valuable support and resources for both victims and offenders:

1. Support for Victims: Community members can provide emotional and practical support to victims throughout the restorative justice process. Their presence can help victims feel heard, valued, and less isolated during a challenging time. This support can be instrumental in the healing process for victims, helping them cope with the trauma of the offense.

2. Encouragement of Accountability: Community involvement reinforces the message that offenses harm not only individual victims but also the broader community. This emphasis on collective accountability can motivate offenders to take their actions more seriously and understand the impact of their behavior on the people they live alongside.

3. Guidance for Offenders: Community members can serve as positive role models and mentors for young offenders. By engaging with them in a supportive and constructive manner, community involvement offers opportunities for rehabilitation and personal growth. Offenders may find guidance and mentorship, which can steer them away from criminal behavior and toward more pro-social choices.

4. Resource Accessibility: Communities often have access to a range of resources, such as counseling services, job training programs, and educational opportunities. These

resources can be invaluable in helping offenders address the underlying causes of their behavior and gain the skills needed to reintegrate successfully into society.

5. Community Restoration: Restorative justice is not just about healing individuals but also restoring the social fabric of communities. Community involvement allows for collective reflection on the harm caused and the measures required to repair that harm. This process fosters a sense of cohesion and unity within the community, which can contribute to increased safety and well-being.

6. Preventing Recidivism: Community support and involvement can be a strong protective factor against recidivism. By providing a sense of belonging and purpose, offenders are less likely to return to criminal behavior, reducing the risk to victims and the community at large.

Communities across the nation are exploring innovative approaches to diminish the reliance on traditional policing. Among these initiatives, there's a growing trend towards civilian-based alternative first-responder programs, particularly in addressing behavioral health crises. These programs have existed for some time, with new proposals emerging to broaden their scope, including responses to quality-of-life concerns and low-level complaints, as well as traffic enforcement. Such community-driven endeavors aim to reduce over-policing, improve service quality, and enhance community safety.

One promising concept involves the utilization of alternative first responders whenever possible. A prime example is the Crisis Assistance Helping Out on the Streets (CAHOOTS) program in Eugene, Oregon. In this model, two-person teams, composed of a mental health crisis worker and an emergency medical technician, respond to a range of 911 and non-emergency calls involving mental health crises, intoxication, substance abuse, and homelessness. CAHOOTS provides voluntary services, including crisis intervention, counseling, and referrals to social services. This approach offers a more suitable and less intimidating response to behavioral health crises compared to traditional police involvement, ultimately mitigating the risk of escalations into police violence. Such alternatives also hold the potential to significantly reduce volatile police-citizen interactions in disadvantaged communities, all while being relatively cost-effective.

Beyond addressing behavioral health crises, civilians may prove to be more effective responders in handling minor complaints, disturbances, disorderly conduct, and quality-of-life concerns. These types of calls constitute a substantial portion of police service requests, with conventional police responses often raising concerns about the use of harsh and racially discriminatory tactics, eroding trust within marginalized communities. Trained community members skilled in de-escalation and mediation might offer a peaceful resolution without police involvement. While the idea of community members responding to 911 calls for quality-of-life concerns is relatively new, engaging trained community members, often known as "violence interrupters," for mediating conflicts has been effective for some time. Given the negative impact of harsh order-maintenance policing on marginalized communities, these areas might contemplate programs redirecting quality-of-life and low-level calls to civilian community responders. The success of behavioral health responder models like CAHOOTS suggests that civilian community responder programs offer a cost-effective way to provide emergency services reliably.

Moreover, several cities are exploring the potential of unarmed civilians, housed within the Department of Transportation, to enforce minor traffic violations. Over-policing is particularly evident in traffic enforcement, with Black and Latino drivers experiencing a higher likelihood of being stopped, searched, cited, and arrested compared to their white counterparts. Minor traffic violations can serve as a pretext for invasive investigatory stops, contributing to a significant percentage of fatal police shootings. Proposals suggest that unarmed traffic monitors could issue citations for minor traffic violations while refraining from conducting background checks or criminal investigations. This approach could notably reduce the frequency of contentious police-civilian encounters, lessening the impact of over-policing in disadvantaged communities.

Other promising programs include community violence-interruption initiatives, such as the Cure Violence model. These programs train and employ community members as outreach workers and violence interrupters, offering credible messengers who can connect with at-risk youth. Violence interrupters work to mediate conflicts and de-escalate potentially violent situations, while outreach workers build long-term relationships with young individuals at risk of criminal involvement, guiding them towards better choices and access to services like education and job training. Additionally, school and community restorative-justice programs are making significant strides in preventing crime without police involvement, particularly in schools where punitive disciplinary measures have disproportionately affected students of color. Restorative-justice circles bring together students and teachers to collaboratively address conflicts and behavioral issues, with early reports indicating a reduction in suspensions, expulsions, and police referrals, improved graduation rates, and decreased racial disparities in discipline.

In the broader community, restorative practices are being employed to steer at-risk individuals away from criminal behavior. Nonprofit organizations and community groups are organizing peacemaking circles and conflict resolution circles, where community members engage in guided conversations on various themes, addressing issues like violence, gang involvement, and goal setting. These programs offer a unique avenue to prevent crime and promote community safety while reducing negative police-civilian interactions. While none of these initiatives eliminates the necessity for police intervention in violent crimes, collectively, they hold the potential to reduce violence, enhance safety, and minimize adverse police-citizen interactions.

In essence, community involvement in restorative justice processes enriches the experience for all parties involved—victims, offenders, and the community itself. It promotes healing, accountability, and rehabilitation while reinforcing the idea that justice is not just a legal process but a communal endeavor focused on restoration and building stronger, more supportive neighborhoods.

CHAPTER 07

RESTORATIVE PRACTICES

Restorative practices encompass a diverse range of methods and approaches aimed at addressing harm, fostering accountability, and promoting healing in juvenile cases. These practices offer an alternative to punitive measures and emphasize dialogue, understanding, and resolution. Several key restorative practices commonly applied in juvenile cases include victim-offender dialogues, circles, and conferences.

Victim-offender dialogues involve a facilitated conversation between the victim and the young offender, where they have the opportunity to discuss the impact of the offense, ask questions, express their feelings, and work together to reach a mutually agreed-upon resolution. This process promotes empathy and helps both parties find closure.

Restorative circles bring together affected parties, including victims, offenders, and community members, in a safe and structured environment. Circles encourage open and honest communication, allowing participants to share their perspectives, address underlying issues, and collaboratively decide on how to repair the harm caused.

Restorative conferences are more formal gatherings that involve trained facilitators. They bring together victims, offenders, their supporters, and relevant community members to discuss the offense, its consequences, and develop a restitution plan or other meaningful ways to make amends.

These restorative practices aim to give victims a voice, hold offenders accountable, and involve the community in the resolution process. They prioritize healing and understanding over punishment, recognizing that addressing the harm caused is key to reducing recidivism and building stronger, more compassionate communities.

Restorative practices for juveniles encompass a range of structured processes and interventions designed to address harm, promote accountability, and facilitate healing among young offenders, victims, and the community. Here are various restorative practices commonly applied in juvenile cases:

1. Victim-Offender Dialogues (VODs): These one-on-one meetings between the victim and the offender are a cornerstone of restorative justice. Facilitated by a trained mediator, VODs provide a safe and structured space for both parties to engage in open and honest communication. Victims have the opportunity to express their feelings, ask questions, and share the impact of the offense, while offenders are encouraged to take responsibility for their actions, express remorse, and work towards making amends. VODs aim to foster empathy, understanding, and the development of a restitution plan.

2. Restorative Circles: Restorative circles are group meetings that bring together the victim, offender, their supporters, and sometimes community members. The process is facilitated by a trained circle keeper who guides the conversation. Restorative circles provide a structured format for participants to discuss the offense, its impact, and potential resolutions. These circles emphasize active listening,

understanding, and collective problem-solving, fostering a sense of community and shared responsibility.

3. Restorative Conferences: Restorative conferences are more formal gatherings that include the victim, offender, their respective supporters, and trained facilitators. They follow a structured agenda, beginning with the victim's perspective and moving towards understanding the offender's actions and motivations. Together, the participants develop a plan for restitution or reconciliation. These conferences often result in a written agreement that outlines the steps the offender will take to make amends.

4. Restitution Plans: Restitution plans are agreements that specify how the offender will make amends for the harm caused. This may include financial restitution to cover damages, community service, participation in educational programs, or other forms of redress. Restitution plans are tailored to the specific circumstances of each case and are developed collaboratively with input from victims, offenders, and the community.

5. Peer Mediation: In some juvenile cases, peer mediation may be used as a restorative practice. Trained peer mediators facilitate conversations between young offenders involved in conflicts or disputes. This approach aims to empower young individuals to resolve conflicts peacefully,

build communication skills, and take responsibility for their actions.

6. Family Group Conferences: Family group conferences involve the extended family and significant others of the young offender. The process centers on collective decision-making and support for the offender's rehabilitation. Family group conferences recognize the role of family dynamics in the juvenile's behavior and aim to harness family resources to address the underlying issues.

Restorative justice encompasses various approaches, but within the criminal context, it commonly involves a gathering of the victim, the offender, and community representatives. In this setting, the offender takes responsibility for the harm caused, and the group collectively determines actions the offender can undertake to mend the harm and prevent further transgressions. Typically, cases are referred to independent nonprofit organizations by police or prosecutors who collaborate with community volunteers to facilitate these restorative processes. The victim's consent is usually a prerequisite for cases to be directed toward restorative justice, and when victims opt out, surrogate victims, often community members who have experienced similar harm, can step in. Defendants may be offered the choice to participate in restorative justice at various stages of the criminal process, either as a diversion from the standard process, an alternative form of sentencing, or even, in more severe cases, as a means to reduce the criminal sentence.

As detailed below, restorative processes have proven to offer victims greater satisfaction compared to the conventional criminal process, effectively holding offenders accountable, reducing recidivism, and often mitigating or eliminating the need for incarceration. The benefits of restorative justice are particularly pertinent for marginalized communities due to several reasons. Firstly, it provides an effective response to harm, thereby alleviating the burden of over-policing and harsh crime control measures on these communities. Secondly, the community-centered and localized nature of restorative justice programs allows communities disproportionately affected by crime and stringent criminal policies to determine the extent to which they wish to incorporate restorative alternatives into their criminal justice system. Lastly, the inclusion of restorative justice programs may enhance the legitimacy of the criminal process, fostering greater community trust.

Restorative justice extends beyond merely being a method for communities to circumvent severe criminal policies. As advocates have emphasized, restorative approaches better address the needs of victims than traditional criminal processes. By affording victims a voice and active participation in the case resolution, restorative processes empower victims, enabling them to regain a sense of control and overcome feelings of powerlessness. In contrast, the conventional criminal process often does little to promote victim healing or reestablish a sense of safety, occasionally even causing psychological harm. Furthermore, restorative-justice proponents point out that victims' desire for safety and justice doesn't necessarily translate into a preference for harsh punishment for offenders. Surveys of crime victims indicate a preference for a justice system focused on rehabilitation over punitive measures, supporting noncustodial forms of accountability, and the belief that imprisonment is more likely to lead to further criminal behavior than rehabilitation.

Empirical research lends weight to the argument that restorative justice offers more to victims than the conventional criminal process. Multiple randomized control studies demonstrate that restorative justice outperforms the standard process on various metrics related to victims' psychological well-being and perceptions of fairness. For instance, a comprehensive study in Australia, spanning several years and covering cases of personal property crime and mid-level violent offenses, revealed significant psychological benefits for victims participating in restorative justice. Victims of violent crimes going through the conventional court process were five times more likely to believe they might be revictimized by the offender compared to those whose cases were referred to restorative justice. The study also found that victims who partook in restorative conferences felt more secure, less anxious, less fearful of the offender, and experienced a greater sense of closure than those whose cases proceeded through the criminal process.

Restorative processes additionally excel in holding offenders accountable, presenting a more direct and meaningful approach compared to criminal punishment. Criminal harm encompasses not only physical and material damage but also the moral or expressive injury inflicted—the offender has shown disregard for the victim's rights and society's rules. While traditional punishment aims to correct this injury through condemnation of the offender's actions, restorative justice focuses on the offender acknowledging the harm and wrong done. It encourages the offender to apologize, express remorse, voluntarily seek to repair the harm, and commit to abiding by societal rules in the future.

In contrast, the adversarial nature of the criminal process often pushes offenders to deny responsibility, as they seldom hear an account of the effect of their actions on the victims. Offenders frequently feel their treatment within the criminal process or the sentences they receive are unjust. This preoccupation with their own mistreatment distracts them from taking responsibility for their actions and experiencing remorse for the harm caused.

Restorative processes are also more effective at rehabilitating and reintegrating offenders. Restorative agreements differ from case to case but generally involve symbolic reparation in the form of an apology, community service, material restitution to address the victim's financial losses, and educational components addressing the impact of the offense. Agreements may also include measures aimed at tackling the root causes of offending, such as mental health or drug treatment, counseling, education, job training, and reflective exercises promoting individual skills like decision-making, goal-setting, and recognizing multiple perspectives, as well as reflection on bias and systemic injustice. Studies indicate that restorative processes do a better job of reducing recidivism than the criminal process, with some research suggesting that this effect is most pronounced for violent offenses and somewhat more significant for adult offenders compared to juveniles.

Crucially, restorative justice can achieve these positive outcomes while minimizing the severe criminal penalties that have had detrimental effects on individuals and communities. For these reasons, disadvantaged communities should have access to community-based restorative justice programs.

These restorative practices are applied in juvenile cases to provide alternatives to punitive methods, emphasize personal responsibility, promote empathy and understanding, and encourage collaborative problem-solving. They offer a more comprehensive and holistic approach to addressing juvenile delinquency, focusing on healing, rehabilitation, and community involvement.

CHAPTER 08

BENEFITS OF RESTORATIVE JUSTICE

The benefits of restorative justice in the context of juvenile cases are profound and far-reaching. One of its primary advantages is the substantial reduction in recidivism rates among young offenders. By addressing the root causes of delinquent behavior and fostering accountability and empathy, restorative justice programs empower juveniles to make positive changes in their lives, ultimately steering them away from a path of reoffending.

Moreover, restorative justice leads to improved victim satisfaction. Victims often find solace and closure in having their voices heard and their needs addressed directly. This contrasts with the often-frustrating experience of navigating the traditional criminal justice system, where the victim's role can be limited to that of a witness.

Restorative justice also strengthens communities. By involving the community in the resolution process, it promotes a sense of shared responsibility and connectedness. This, in turn, fosters safer and more supportive neighborhoods, where individuals are more likely to cooperate in preventing further delinquency and addressing the broader social issues that contribute to juvenile crime.

Additionally, restorative justice can lead to cost savings for the justice system. By reducing recidivism rates, it decreases the burden on correctional facilities and court systems, ultimately making more efficient use of resources.

In sum, the benefits of restorative justice for juveniles extend beyond individual cases to encompass reduced reoffending, increased victim satisfaction, and the creation of stronger, more resilient communities that prioritize healing and accountability over punitive measures.

Restorative justice for juveniles offers a range of benefits that extend beyond traditional punitive methods.

These positive outcomes contribute to the well-being of young offenders, victims, and the broader community. Here are some key benefits:

1. Reduced Recidivism Rates: Restorative justice has been shown to be effective in reducing recidivism among young offenders. By addressing the underlying causes of delinquent behavior, promoting accountability, and fostering personal growth, restorative practices help break the cycle of criminal behavior. Young offenders who go through restorative processes are less likely to reoffend compared to those subjected to traditional punitive measures.

2. Improved Victim Satisfaction: Victims often express higher levels of satisfaction with the restorative justice process compared to traditional court proceedings. Restorative practices provide victims with an opportunity to be heard, ask questions, and actively participate in shaping the resolution. This empowerment and engagement can lead to a greater sense of justice and closure for victims.

3. Healing and Emotional Recovery: Restorative justice processes prioritize the emotional and psychological needs of victims. By allowing victims to express their feelings and receive answers to their questions, these processes can contribute to healing and emotional recovery. Victims may

experience a reduction in trauma-related symptoms and an increased sense of safety.

4. Accountability and Responsibility: Restorative justice places a strong emphasis on accountability and personal responsibility for young offenders. Through victim-offender dialogues, restitution plans, and other practices, offenders are encouraged to take ownership of their actions and actively work towards making amends. This accountability promotes self-reflection and growth.

5. Community Building: Restorative justice actively involves the community in the resolution process, fostering a sense of collective responsibility for addressing harm. By participating in circles, conferences, or other practices, community members can strengthen social bonds, trust, and cooperation. This sense of community can contribute to safer and more cohesive neighborhoods.

6. Enhanced Communication and Empathy: Restorative processes facilitate open and honest communication between victims and offenders. This communication fosters empathy, allowing both parties to better understand each other's perspectives and needs. The development of empathy can lead to improved relationships and a reduced likelihood of future conflicts.

7. Prevention of Secondary Victimization: Restorative justice processes aim to prevent re-victimization by ensuring that victims are treated with dignity and respect throughout the process. This reduces the risk of secondary trauma that can result from traditional court proceedings.

8. Personal Growth and Rehabilitation: Restorative justice offers young offenders an opportunity for personal growth and rehabilitation. By addressing the root causes of their behavior and providing access to support services, counseling, and educational opportunities, restorative practices aim to help offenders reintegrate into society as responsible citizens.

Effective communication with the community is a fundamental prerequisite for the success of a restorative justice program. Communities may initially hold reservations regarding the program's impact and legitimacy. Addressing these concerns in public communications is essential. Moreover, it is imperative to engage with community members as their concerns arise, inviting their active participation and involvement in the program. This inclusive approach fosters a broad foundation of support for the initiative. Maintaining open lines of communication through regular consultations and information sharing further ensures a positive community disposition toward the program.

Typically, communication with the community is facilitated through the mass media. Collaborating with the media to elucidate the program's purpose and keep the community informed of its progress is of paramount importance. Negative and fear-inducing stories can lead to unfavorable press, resulting in a decline in public perception. This, in turn, can discourage other agencies from referring cases to the program.

Successful programs often implement comprehensive communication plans founded on honesty and transparency. While privacy considerations may occasionally limit transparency, avoiding hyperbolic public statements, unjustified criticisms of other agencies, or exaggerated claims about program success is crucial. Instead, the focus should be on presenting accurate facts and genuine human stories that the public can relate to. Engaging community opinion leaders and spokespersons from other justice agencies to publicly express their support for the program can further bolster its credibility.

Furthermore, every program should have a contingency communication plan readily available for implementation in the event that a case goes awry or an offender involved attracts negative attention to the program. Anticipating that there will be at least one problematic case in the future, programs should be prepared to handle these situations effectively to ensure their continued success and credibility.

CHAPTER 09

CHALLENGES AND CRITICISM

While restorative justice holds promise, it is not without its share of challenges and criticisms. One of the primary concerns relates to issues of fairness and equity. Critics argue that the success of restorative justice heavily depends on the willingness and motivation of all parties involved, which can lead to unequal outcomes. Some victims may feel pressured into participating, while others may not have access to the resources or support needed to engage effectively.

Effectiveness is another point of contention. While restorative justice has shown success in reducing recidivism rates for certain offenses, its applicability to more serious or violent crimes is questioned. Critics argue that it may not be suitable for cases where safety concerns are paramount, as it relies heavily on open dialogue between victims and offenders.

Another criticism pertains to the potential for retraumatization of victims. In some cases, the victim-offender dialogue may inadvertently reopen emotional wounds or exacerbate trauma, which is a significant concern.

Additionally, concerns about consistency and standardization exist. Restorative justice programs can vary widely in their implementation, which raises questions about the consistency of outcomes and the potential for unintended consequences.

It's essential to acknowledge these criticisms and challenges in the practice of restorative justice for juveniles while working to address them and refine the approach to make it as fair, effective, and safe as possible.

While restorative justice holds promise as a more compassionate and effective approach to addressing juvenile delinquency, it is not without its challenges and criticisms. It's important to acknowledge these concerns and consider how they can be addressed:

1. Fairness and Equity Concerns:

   - Selectivity: Critics argue that restorative justice may not be applied consistently or fairly, leading to concerns about selectivity in choosing which cases go through restorative processes. This selectivity can result in disparities in treatment among young offenders.

   - Power Imbalance: Some critics suggest that there can be a power imbalance in restorative justice processes, particularly when victims and offenders have differing levels of support or resources. Ensuring that all parties are on equal footing can be challenging.

2. Victim Participation:

   - Pressure to Participate: There may be pressure on victims to participate in restorative processes, which could potentially retraumatize them or make them uncomfortable. Ensuring that participation is entirely voluntary and that victims are fully informed about their rights and options is crucial.

   - Victim Empowerment: While restorative justice aims to empower victims, there can be cases where victims feel overwhelmed by the process or not adequately supported. Providing resources and support for victims is essential.

3. Offender Accountability:

- Genuine Accountability: Critics question whether offenders in restorative justice processes truly take responsibility for their actions or if they engage merely to avoid harsher consequences. Ensuring that accountability is genuine and not coerced is a significant challenge.

- Reoffending Risk: Some worry that restorative justice may not effectively deter offenders from reoffending, especially when compared to traditional punitive measures. Ensuring that rehabilitation and support services are provided to address the root causes of delinquency is crucial to reducing reoffending.

4. Resource Limitations:

- Training and Implementation: Implementing restorative justice programs effectively requires trained facilitators and resources, which can be a challenge in communities with limited funding and capacity.

- Monitoring and Evaluation: Assessing the effectiveness of restorative justice programs requires resources for data collection and evaluation, which some communities may struggle to allocate.

5. Cultural Sensitivity:

- Cultural Awareness: Restorative justice programs must be culturally sensitive and adaptable to the diverse communities they serve. Ensuring that processes are respectful of cultural differences can be challenging and requires ongoing education and training.

6. Ensuring Safety:

- Safety Concerns: There can be safety concerns when bringing victims and offenders together, particularly in cases of violent or deeply traumatizing offenses. Ensuring the safety and emotional well-being of all participants is essential.

7. Limited Applicability:

- Suitability of Cases: Restorative justice may not be suitable for all cases, particularly those involving repeat or violent offenders. Identifying which cases are appropriate for restorative processes is a challenge.

Several challenges arise when attempting to evaluate the effectiveness of restorative justice processes. These challenges encompass, but are not limited to, the following factors:

1. Securing Adequate Control Groups: Difficulty in finding suitable control groups of crime victims and offenders who underwent traditional criminal justice procedures for comparison.

2. Diversity of Restorative Programs: The wide range of restorative programs available, each with its own set of goals and objectives.

3. Variability Among Programs: Substantial variability among restorative programs concerning the nature and volume of cases processed.

4. Inadequate Controls and Comparability: The absence of adequate controls and comparability in areas such as referral criteria, facilitator competence and training, legislative and policy frameworks, and outcome benchmarks.

5. Variable Indicators: Differences in the indicators used to measure program success.

6. Recidivism Assessment Periods: Variations in the time periods used to assess recidivism among offenders participating in restorative programs.

7. Assessment of Satisfaction and Fear: Diverse measures and indicators used to evaluate crime victim and offender satisfaction, fear levels among victims, and expectations of both parties regarding the restorative process.

8. Subjective Assessment Methods: The subjective and personal nature of processes involved in restorative justice.

9. Community Contexts: The need to account for diverse contexts in which restorative processes operate, such as urban or rural settings, and highly troubled or highly integrated communities.

10. Staff Training Variability: Differences in the types of training provided to program staff and facilitators.

11. Legislative and Policy Frameworks: Variances in the legislative and policy frameworks within which restorative processes are implemented.

12. Quantifying Subjective Experiences: The challenge of quantifying subjective, personal, and interactive aspects of restorative justice.

13. Assessing Capacity Enhancement: Developing measures to assess the extent to which restorative processes enhance community, family, and system capacities.

14. Victim Empowerment and Offender Rehabilitation: Creating measures to assess victim empowerment, offender remorse, and rehabilitation.

15. Operationalizing Abstract Concepts: Defining and measuring abstract concepts like "community capacity," "family capacity," "system capacity," "victim empowerment," and "community engagement."

16. Cost-Effectiveness Analysis: Developing measures to assess the cost-effectiveness of restorative justice initiatives, especially in comparison to traditional criminal justice systems.

Moreover, existing evaluations primarily focus on the experiences of crime victims and offenders, while offering less insight into the perspectives of politicians, senior law enforcement, and criminal justice personnel. These decision-makers have a substantial impact on the development, implementation, and overall success of restorative justice processes. Similarly, little attention has been given to the role of facilitators in the success of restorative practices, including their training, personality, style, and experience in achieving positive outcomes. The experience of the process by crime victims and offenders is influenced by factors like legislative and policy contexts and facilitator skills, in addition to the specific restorative approach used.

To meet rigorous evaluation standards, it's essential to compare the experiences and attitudes of a group of offenders and victims who participated in a restorative process with a matched group who underwent the standard criminal justice response.

Addressing these challenges and criticisms requires careful planning, ongoing evaluation, and a commitment to fairness, equity, and the well-being of all participants. Restorative justice programs must be implemented with sensitivity to the unique needs and circumstances of each case and community to ensure their effectiveness and legitimacy.

CHAPTER 10

LEGAL FRAMEWORK

The legal framework for implementing restorative justice for juveniles is a critical aspect of its integration into the criminal justice system. In many jurisdictions, restorative justice programs operate within existing legal systems, often as complementary processes rather than replacements.

Typically, this framework involves legislation that authorizes the use of restorative justice practices in juvenile cases. It outlines the types of offenses eligible for restorative justice, the rights and roles of victims and offenders, and the procedures for conducting restorative processes. It may also establish the qualifications and training requirements for facilitators and practitioners.

Importantly, this legal framework ensures that restorative justice practices adhere to due process and respect the legal rights of all parties involved. It provides safeguards to prevent coercion or manipulation during victim-offender dialogues or conferences.

Restorative justice programs often collaborate closely with juvenile courts, probation services, and other legal entities. They are integrated into the broader juvenile justice system, allowing for referrals to restorative processes as an alternative or adjunct to traditional court proceedings. In cases where an agreement is reached through restorative means, the legal framework may stipulate how this agreement is enforced and the consequences for non-compliance.

By aligning restorative justice with existing legal systems, the framework seeks to strike a balance between promoting rehabilitation, accountability, and the protection of rights within the context of juvenile cases. This integration acknowledges the importance of providing a comprehensive and fair approach to address juvenile delinquency.

The legal framework for implementing restorative justice for juveniles varies from one jurisdiction to another, but there are common elements that can be considered when integrating restorative justice practices into existing legal systems. Here's an overview of the legal framework for juvenile restorative justice:

1. Legislation and Policy: To establish a legal framework for juvenile restorative justice, jurisdictions often enact legislation or develop policy guidelines that explicitly recognize and support restorative justice practices. This legislation should define the scope, purpose, and principles of restorative justice for juveniles and may include provisions for confidentiality, victim participation, and offender rights.

2. Referral Mechanisms: A critical aspect of the legal framework is establishing clear referral mechanisms for cases that are appropriate for restorative justice processes. This typically involves collaboration between law enforcement, juvenile justice agencies, prosecutors, and the judiciary to identify eligible cases and refer them to restorative justice programs.

3. Informed Consent: Ensuring that all parties, including victims and offenders, provide informed and voluntary consent to participate in restorative justice processes is essential. Legal frameworks should outline the informed consent process, emphasizing that participation is not coerced.

4. Rights Protections: Legal frameworks must protect the rights of both victims and offenders during restorative justice processes. This includes ensuring that victims are informed of their rights, such as the right to refuse participation, and that offenders have due process rights, such as the right to legal representation.

5. Confidentiality: Establishing rules and legal safeguards to protect the confidentiality of information shared during restorative justice processes is crucial. This helps create a safe and open environment for all participants.

6. Documentation and Records: Legal frameworks should specify the documentation and record-keeping requirements for restorative justice cases. This includes maintaining records of agreements reached, restitution plans, and outcomes.

7. Enforceability: Agreements and outcomes reached through restorative justice processes should be legally enforceable. This means that if an offender fails to fulfill their obligations, there are mechanisms in place to ensure compliance, potentially through the traditional justice system.

8. Training and Accreditation: Legal frameworks may require training and accreditation for individuals involved in restorative justice processes, such as mediators and

facilitators. This ensures that the process is conducted professionally and ethically.

9. Evaluation and Oversight: Legal frameworks should establish mechanisms for ongoing evaluation and oversight of restorative justice programs to assess their effectiveness, adherence to established guidelines, and overall impact on recidivism and victim satisfaction.

10. Community Collaboration: Legal frameworks may encourage or require collaboration between justice agencies, community organizations, and service providers to support the successful implementation of restorative justice programs.

Incorporating restorative justice into the legal framework for juvenile justice allows for a more balanced and comprehensive approach to addressing juvenile delinquency. It complements existing punitive measures with a focus on healing, rehabilitation, and community involvement, ultimately contributing to the well-being of young offenders and the communities they are part of.

CHAPTER 11

CASE STUDIES

Case studies hold a pivotal role in elucidating the effectiveness and real-world impact of restorative justice in juvenile cases. These real-life narratives serve as compelling examples of how restorative practices can transform lives and communities.

One case study might revolve around a young offender who, through a restorative process, not only takes responsibility for their actions but also gains insight into the harm caused to the victim. Over time, they make amends, complete their education, and secure employment, illustrating the power of rehabilitation and personal growth within the restorative justice framework.

Another case study could feature a victim who finds closure and healing through a restorative conference, giving them a sense of justice that they might not have achieved through traditional court proceedings. Such stories underscore the importance of giving victims a voice and involving them in the resolution process.

Additionally, case studies can highlight reduced recidivism rates within communities that have adopted restorative justice approaches. They demonstrate how these practices contribute to safer and more cohesive neighborhoods, ultimately benefiting society as a whole.

These real-life examples not only showcase the potential of restorative justice but also provide valuable insights and inspiration for practitioners, policymakers, and the public. They illustrate that, when implemented effectively, restorative justice can be a powerful force for positive change in the lives of young offenders and the communities they are part of.

Case studies play a crucial role in illustrating the practical application and effectiveness of restorative justice in juvenile cases. They provide real-life examples of how restorative justice principles and practices can lead to positive outcomes for young offenders, victims, and communities. Here are a few case studies that highlight the importance of such examples:

1. The Peacemaking Circle in a School Setting:

- Case: In a middle school, a student named Alex had been repeatedly involved in conflicts and disruptive behavior. Instead of resorting to suspension or expulsion, the school implemented a restorative justice approach. A peacemaking circle was convened with Alex, his classmates, and a trained facilitator. They discussed the underlying issues, such as bullying and peer pressure, that contributed to Alex's behavior.

- Outcome: Through the circle, Alex gained insight into the harm he had caused and developed empathy for his classmates. He agreed to make amends by organizing anti-bullying workshops and participating in conflict resolution training. The school saw a significant reduction in disciplinary incidents involving Alex, and he became an advocate for positive change in his school community.

2. Victim-Offender Dialogue in a Youth Offender Case:

- Case: A 16-year-old named Sarah had shoplifted from a local store, causing distress to the store owner. Instead of pursuing charges through the juvenile court system, the victim and Sarah's guardian agreed to a victim-offender dialogue facilitated by a restorative justice practitioner.

- Outcome: During the dialogue, Sarah apologized to the store owner and learned about the financial and emotional impact of her actions. The store owner, in turn, expressed his concerns and expectations. Together, they agreed on a restitution plan, which involved Sarah completing community service and writing a letter of apology. The victim felt heard and satisfied with the resolution, and Sarah gained insight into the consequences of her actions. She successfully completed her restitution plan and did not reoffend.

3. Community Conference for a Group of Juvenile Offenders:

- Case: In a neighborhood with high rates of youth gang involvement, a series of property crimes, vandalism, and minor assaults were committed by a group of young offenders. The community and law enforcement decided to hold a restorative justice community conference involving the offenders, victims, community members, and service providers.

- Outcome: During the conference, the young offenders heard directly from the victims about the impact of their actions on the community's sense of safety. The offenders agreed to participate in community improvement projects, attend conflict resolution workshops, and engage in mentorship programs. Over time, the community saw a reduction in youth-related crime, and the young offenders became actively involved in community initiatives, steering them away from further criminal behavior.

Case studies like these demonstrate the practical benefits of restorative justice in addressing juvenile delinquency. They show how restorative practices can lead to personal growth, accountability, victim satisfaction, and safer, more cohesive communities. By highlighting these real-life examples, restorative justice advocates can inspire others to consider and implement these principles and practices in their own communities.

CHAPTER 12

RESTORATIVE JUSTICE WORLDWIDE

Restorative justice practices have gained recognition and acceptance on a global scale, yet their implementation varies significantly across different countries and cultures. While some nations have embraced restorative principles as a fundamental component of their justice systems, others are still in the early stages of adopting or experimenting with these practices.

In countries like New Zealand and several Scandinavian nations, restorative justice has been integrated extensively into their legal systems. These countries emphasize community involvement, victim-offender dialogues, and rehabilitation, leading to lower recidivism rates and increased victim satisfaction.

In contrast, other countries, including some in Asia and the Middle East, may have cultural or legal barriers that hinder the full-scale implementation of restorative justice. Traditional notions of justice, notions of retribution, and a lack of awareness about restorative principles can be significant challenges.

International perspectives on restorative justice also highlight the importance of adapting these practices to fit cultural norms and legal frameworks. What works well in one country may require modifications to be effective in another. The diversity of global approaches underscores the need for ongoing dialogue and the exchange of best practices to ensure that restorative justice continues to evolve and make a positive impact worldwide.

While the extent of restorative justice implementation varies, its core principles of accountability, empathy, and community involvement continue to resonate across diverse cultures, offering hope for more compassionate and effective approaches to juvenile justice on a global scale.

The effectiveness of juvenile restorative justice practices worldwide varies significantly depending on the jurisdiction, cultural context, and the level of implementation and support for these practices. Here's an overview of the effectiveness of juvenile restorative justice on a global scale, along with some international perspectives:

1. Varying Levels of Implementation:

- The adoption and implementation of juvenile restorative justice practices differ from country to country. Some nations have well-established restorative justice programs integrated into their juvenile justice systems, while others are just beginning to explore these approaches.

2. Cultural Sensitivity and Acceptance:

- The effectiveness of restorative justice often depends on the cultural acceptance and appropriateness of these practices. In some cultures, restorative approaches align well with traditional dispute resolution mechanisms and community values, making them more effective and readily accepted. In other cultures, the introduction of restorative justice may face resistance or skepticism.

3. Impact on Recidivism:

- Research suggests that restorative justice programs can be effective in reducing recidivism among young offenders when properly implemented. However, the degree of effectiveness may vary depending on the program's quality, duration, and the specific needs of the participants.

4. Victim Satisfaction:

- Restorative justice is often associated with higher levels of victim satisfaction compared to traditional punitive approaches. When victims feel heard, empowered, and involved in the resolution process, they are more likely to report a positive experience.

5. Community Engagement:

- The extent to which communities are engaged in restorative justice processes can influence their effectiveness. In some countries, strong community involvement contributes to the success of restorative programs by providing support, resources, and a sense of collective responsibility.

6. Legal Framework and Policy Support:

- The presence of a legal framework and policy support for restorative justice can greatly affect its effectiveness. Countries with well-defined legislation and policies that support restorative justice tend to have more successful implementation and higher levels of accountability.

7. Challenges and Barriers:
   - Challenges to the effectiveness of juvenile restorative justice practices can include resource limitations, lack of training, concerns about fairness, and difficulties in engaging all parties involved, especially in cases of serious offenses.

   International Perspectives:
   - New Zealand: New Zealand has a well-established restorative justice program called Family Group Conferencing (FGC). FGC is a central component of their juvenile justice system and has been credited with reducing recidivism rates and improving outcomes for both victims and offenders.

   - Norway: Norway places a strong emphasis on rehabilitation in its juvenile justice system, which aligns with restorative principles. The country's approach focuses on providing support, education, and therapeutic interventions to young offenders, with an emphasis on reintegrating them into society as responsible citizens.

   - Canada: Canada has integrated restorative justice practices into its juvenile justice system, recognizing the importance of addressing the needs of indigenous youth. Restorative justice initiatives have been successful in promoting reconciliation and reducing the overrepresentation of indigenous youth in the criminal justice system.

- Australia: Restorative justice programs, including conferencing, are used in various parts of Australia's juvenile justice system. These programs aim to address the unique needs of indigenous youth and have shown promise in reducing recidivism and enhancing victim satisfaction.

In summary, the effectiveness of juvenile restorative justice practices varies worldwide and is influenced by a range of factors, including cultural context, legal frameworks, community engagement, and the level of support and resources available. While restorative justice can be a valuable and effective approach in many contexts, its impact may differ from one jurisdiction to another, underscoring the importance of considering local and cultural factors when implementing these practices.

CHAPTER 13

FUTURE DIRECTIONS

The future of restorative justice for juveniles holds exciting possibilities for expansion and refinement. One promising direction is the further integration of restorative justice into existing juvenile justice systems. As awareness of its benefits grows, more jurisdictions may adopt and institutionalize these practices as a primary approach to handling young offenders.

Technological advancements also offer opportunities for growth. Online platforms and virtual conferencing can facilitate victim-offender dialogues, making these processes more accessible and convenient, especially in cases where geographical barriers exist.

Enhancing research and data collection is essential for the future of restorative justice. Continued studies can provide insights into which restorative practices are most effective for different types of juvenile offenses and under various circumstances. This research can guide the development of evidence-based programs and best practices.

Additionally, restorative justice can be more inclusive in addressing the diverse needs of juveniles, considering factors such as mental health, substance abuse, and trauma. Tailoring interventions to address these underlying issues can contribute to more comprehensive rehabilitation.

Ultimately, the future of restorative justice for juveniles lies in its ability to evolve, adapt, and address the ever-changing needs of young offenders and their communities. As it continues to demonstrate its potential in reducing recidivism, promoting healing, and strengthening communities, restorative justice is poised to play an increasingly pivotal role in shaping the future of juvenile justice worldwide.

The future directions of juvenile restorative justice practices are promising, with the potential for expansion and improvement in various aspects. As societies continue to recognize the value of restorative approaches, here are some potential directions for the development of juvenile restorative justice programs:

1. Integration into Mainstream Juvenile Justice Systems:

   - Many jurisdictions are working towards fully integrating restorative justice practices into their mainstream juvenile justice systems. This involves not only expanding the availability of restorative programs but also ensuring they are recognized and supported by legislative and policy frameworks.

2. Early Intervention and Diversion Programs:

   - Expanding restorative justice to include early intervention and diversion programs can help prevent young individuals from becoming deeply entrenched in the criminal justice system. These programs aim to address minor offenses and conflicts at an early stage, reducing the likelihood of further involvement in criminal activities.

3. Customization and Tailored Approaches:

   - Future directions may involve tailoring restorative justice practices to meet the unique needs of different communities, cultures, and populations, including indigenous youth. Customized approaches can ensure that restorative justice is culturally sensitive and appropriate.

4. Research and Evidence-Based Practices:
   - Continued research and evaluation of restorative justice programs are essential to improving their effectiveness. Future developments should focus on evidence-based practices that demonstrate positive outcomes, including reductions in recidivism and increased victim satisfaction.

5. Technology and Accessibility:
   - Technology can play a significant role in making restorative justice more accessible. Virtual platforms and online tools can facilitate communication between parties, making it easier for participants to engage in restorative processes, particularly in cases where physical presence is challenging.

6. Community Empowerment:
   - Restorative justice should continue to empower communities to take an active role in the resolution of juvenile offenses. This includes community-led initiatives, support networks, and partnerships with local organizations to address the root causes of delinquency.

7. Restorative Education in Schools:
   - Incorporating restorative justice principles and practices into school curricula can help educate young people about conflict resolution, empathy, and accountability. This

preventive approach can contribute to a reduction in school-based conflicts and delinquent behavior.

8. Victim Services and Support:

- Future developments should focus on providing comprehensive victim services and support throughout the restorative justice process. This includes ensuring that victims have access to counseling, legal guidance, and resources to aid their recovery.

9. International Collaboration and Exchange:

- International collaboration and the exchange of best practices can facilitate the global growth of restorative justice. Nations can learn from one another's experiences and adapt successful approaches to their own contexts.

10. Restorative Legislation and Policy Reform:

- Advocates for restorative justice should continue to push for legislative and policy reform that strengthens and supports these practices. Clear legal frameworks can ensure consistency, fairness, and accountability.

11. Cross-Sector Collaboration:

- Collaboration across sectors, including education, social services, and mental health, can help address the underlying causes of juvenile delinquency and enhance the effectiveness of restorative justice programs.

The future of juvenile restorative justice practices lies in their continued evolution, adaptation to diverse contexts, and alignment with the values of healing, accountability, and community involvement. By expanding and improving these programs, societies can work towards a more compassionate and effective approach to addressing juvenile delinquency and promoting the well-being of young offenders, victims, and communities.

CHAPTER 14

PRACTICAL GUIDANCE

Certainly, practical guidance is essential for those interested in implementing restorative justice programs for juveniles. Here are some key steps and considerations for individuals, professionals, and policymakers:

1. Education and Training: Individuals and professionals should seek training and education in restorative justice principles and practices. Numerous organizations and institutions offer courses and resources to build the necessary skills and knowledge.

2. Community Buy-In: Engage with the local community and stakeholders to garner support for restorative justice programs. Building awareness and understanding is crucial for successful implementation.

3. Legal Framework: Policymakers should work on developing or revising legislation that supports the use of restorative justice in juvenile cases. This includes defining the scope of eligible offenses and ensuring due process.

4. Program Design: Tailor restorative justice programs to the specific needs and resources of the community. Consider factors like the size of the population, the availability of trained facilitators, and cultural considerations.

5. Partnerships: Collaborate with existing criminal justice agencies, social services, and community organizations to ensure a coordinated approach. This includes referring cases to restorative justice processes when appropriate.

6. Evaluation and Research: Continuously assess the effectiveness of restorative justice programs through data collection and evaluation. This information can guide improvements and demonstrate the impact of these practices.

7. Support for Victims: Ensure that victims have access to support services, counseling, and legal advice throughout the restorative justice process.

8. Safeguarding Rights: Maintain a strong focus on protecting the rights and well-being of all participants, including offenders. Facilitators should be trained in ensuring a fair and safe process.

9. Restitution Plans: Develop clear guidelines for creating restitution plans that are meaningful, achievable, and tailored to the needs of victims and the circumstances of offenders.

10. Cultural Sensitivity: Recognize and respect cultural diversity in your community and adapt restorative practices accordingly to ensure inclusivity and effectiveness.

11. Community Building: Beyond individual cases, foster community cohesion and involvement through restorative practices. Encourage volunteerism and participation in restorative justice initiatives.

12. Public Awareness: Invest in public awareness campaigns to educate the community about the benefits of restorative justice and its potential to create safer and more empathetic neighborhoods.

By following these practical guidelines, individuals, professionals, and policymakers can contribute to the successful implementation and growth of restorative justice programs for juveniles, ultimately promoting rehabilitation, accountability, and stronger, more compassionate communities.

Implementing restorative justice programs for juveniles requires careful planning, commitment, and collaboration. Here is practical guidance for individuals, professionals, and policymakers interested in establishing or improving such programs:

For Individuals and Community Members:

1. Education and Training: Educate yourself about restorative justice principles and practices through workshops, seminars, or online resources. Consider becoming a trained facilitator or volunteer in existing restorative programs.

2. Advocacy and Support: Advocate for the implementation of restorative justice in your community, especially for cases involving young offenders. Join or support local organizations and initiatives that promote restorative justice.

3. Community Engagement: Engage with local schools, community centers, and law enforcement agencies to encourage the adoption of restorative practices. Foster dialogue and partnerships to expand the reach of restorative justice.

4. Restorative Values: Promote restorative values such as empathy, accountability, and respect in your personal and community interactions. Encourage others to embrace these values as well.

5. Victim and Offender Support: Offer support and resources to victims and offenders who have gone through restorative processes, helping them reintegrate into the community and access necessary services.

For Professionals and Practitioners:

1. Training and Certification: Pursue formal training and certification in restorative justice practices, such as mediation or facilitation. Continuous professional development ensures you are well-equipped to facilitate restorative processes effectively.

2. Collaboration: Collaborate with other professionals, including social workers, counselors, and educators, to provide comprehensive support to young offenders and victims involved in restorative justice cases.

3. Cultural Competence: Develop cultural competence to ensure that restorative justice processes are respectful and inclusive of diverse backgrounds and identities.

4. Assessment and Evaluation: Establish mechanisms for assessing the effectiveness of your restorative justice

program. Collect data, seek feedback from participants, and use this information to make improvements.

5. Community Outreach: Actively engage with the community to raise awareness of restorative justice benefits and principles. Foster partnerships with local organizations, schools, and justice agencies.

For Policymakers and Government Officials:

1. Legislation and Policy Development: Advocate for the development and implementation of legislation and policies that support restorative justice, including clear guidelines for referrals, informed consent, and enforceability of agreements.

2. Resource Allocation: Allocate resources to support the training of professionals and the establishment of restorative justice programs. Ensure funding for research and evaluation of program effectiveness.

3. Cross-Agency Collaboration: Promote interagency collaboration between juvenile justice, education, and social services departments to create a holistic approach to youth rehabilitation.

4. Community Involvement: Encourage the active involvement of community members in shaping and implementing restorative justice initiatives. Create mechanisms for community input and oversight.

5. Data Collection and Evaluation: Establish data collection and evaluation processes to assess the impact of restorative justice programs on recidivism rates, victim satisfaction, and community safety.

6. Youth Diversion Programs: Develop and support diversion programs that incorporate restorative justice practices as an alternative to traditional court processing for juvenile offenders.

7. Training and Capacity Building: Invest in the training and capacity building of justice system personnel, including judges, prosecutors, and probation officers, to ensure they understand and support restorative justice practices.

8. Public Awareness: Launch public awareness campaigns to educate the public, including young people, about the benefits of restorative justice and the available resources.

By following these practical guidance suggestions, individuals, professionals, and policymakers can contribute to the growth and success of restorative justice programs for juveniles. These efforts can help create a more compassionate and effective juvenile justice system focused on rehabilitation, accountability, and community well-being.

CHAPTER 15

CONCLUSION

In conclusion, this book has journeyed through the transformative realm of restorative justice for juveniles, uncovering its core principles, practices, and profound benefits. We've explored its historical roots and its emergence as a compassionate alternative to punitive methods. We've delved into its victim-centered nature, its focus on offender rehabilitation, and its reliance on community involvement.

Restorative justice, as we've seen, has the power to reduce recidivism rates, improve victim satisfaction, and build stronger, more resilient communities. It stands as a beacon of hope within the criminal justice landscape, offering young offenders a chance for redemption and growth.

As we close these pages, it is crucial to emphasize that restorative justice is not merely a concept; it is a call to action. It beckons us all, individuals, professionals, and policymakers, to champion its cause. By doing so, we can usher in a more compassionate and effective approach to juvenile justice, one that prioritizes healing, accountability, and the forging of stronger, more empathetic communities. In this endeavor, we have the power to transform not only the lives of young offenders but also the very fabric of our society, moving towards a future where restoration and reconciliation hold sway over retribution.

Conclusion: Promoting Restorative Justice for Young Offenders

In the pages of this book, we have embarked on a journey to explore the world of restorative justice for young offenders, a path that leads us towards a more compassionate and effective approach to juvenile justice. As we conclude our exploration, let us reflect on the key takeaways and the importance of promoting restorative justice for our youth:

1. Restorative Justice Principles: Restorative justice centers around principles such as accountability, empathy,

and community involvement. It offers an alternative to traditional punitive methods, focusing on healing, rehabilitation, and reintegration.

2. Victim-Centered Approach: Restorative justice empowers victims by giving them a voice in the process of addressing harm. It prioritizes their healing and satisfaction, offering them the opportunity to be heard and participate in shaping the resolution.

3. Offender Rehabilitation: This approach seeks to rehabilitate young offenders and help them reintegrate into society as responsible citizens. It recognizes that many juvenile offenders have underlying issues that can be addressed through support and intervention.

4. Community Involvement: Communities play a vital role in restorative justice processes, providing support, resources, and a sense of collective responsibility. Engaging the community fosters trust and cooperation.

5. Restorative Practices: Various restorative practices, including victim-offender dialogues, circles, and conferences, offer structured ways to address harm and promote accountability and healing.

6. Benefits: Restorative justice yields positive outcomes, including reduced recidivism rates, improved

victim satisfaction, and stronger communities. It offers a more holistic and balanced approach to juvenile justice.

7. Challenges and Criticisms: While promising, restorative justice faces challenges, including concerns about fairness, equity, and effectiveness. These challenges must be addressed through careful planning and ongoing evaluation.

8. Legal Framework: Establishing a legal framework is essential for the successful implementation of restorative justice. It ensures accountability, informed consent, and enforceability of agreements.

9. Case Studies: Real-life case studies illustrate the transformative power of restorative justice, showcasing how it can lead to personal growth, accountability, and community healing.

10. Global Perspectives: Restorative justice practices vary across different countries and cultures, reflecting the importance of cultural sensitivity and adaptability.

11. Future Directions: The future of juvenile restorative justice holds promise. Expansion, customization, and integration into mainstream systems are on the horizon, along with a focus on early intervention and evidence-based practices.

12. Practical Guidance: Individuals, professionals, and policymakers can contribute to the success of restorative

justice by seeking education, advocating for change, and fostering community engagement.

In conclusion, restorative justice is not just a concept but a path towards a more compassionate and effective approach for young offenders. It emphasizes healing, accountability, and community involvement, providing hope for a brighter future for our youth and our communities. As we move forward, let us continue to champion the cause of restorative justice, for it is a path that leads us towards a more just, empathetic, and united society.